From Obscurity to Oblivion

Collected Poems 2008 –2017

Daniel W. Wright

Spartan
Press

Spartan Press

Kansas City, Missouri

spartanpresskc.com

Spartan
Press

Cover photo: Buzz Wall

Title page drawing: Brandon Barnes

Author photo: Lilly Everett

The author wishes to acknowledge the following: Emily Ebeling, James McDonnell, Brandon Barnes, and the regulars of the Livery Company. Without that place in time, I would not be the writer that I am.

The early literary scene in South City. To Denmark Laine, RC Patterson, Aiko Tsuchida, Cierra Lowe, Hart L'Ecuyer, and Grace McGinnis, I love you all. To Deana Heigl, thanks for being the momma bear to us all. We miss you.

Bad Jacket who took a chance on my writing before anybody else. You showed us all that we were a worth a damn.

My family who showed me the value of hard work and the humor in the darkness the world has to offer. To my mother and grandmother who never gave up on me. To my stepfather who told me early (and often) that I was no good at manual labor.

Venice Café, who gave me a shot. Fred Friction who showed that trial by fire makes better artists of us all. Tracy Swigert and Shameless Grounds for letting artists get weird to find themselves along the way.

Cherokee Street. I've seen this street evolve over fifteen years, and it's always felt like home.

The amazing artists I have met across this country and the world over. You know who you are and I can't wait to see you again.

Finally, to all those who have read my work over the years, thank you so much. I hope you enjoy this and what is yet to come.

-Love, Daniel W. Wright

Table of Contents

Introduction

Daniel W. Wright's latest book of poetry, *From Obscurity to Oblivion: Collected Poems 2008-2017*, stands as a necessary prequel to his established oeuvre. If his previous poetic works were Wright's stoic, calloused, sore thumbs stuck defiantly up to wind, this collection is the hammer smashing flesh and bone. Wright reveals the tragic origin of his romantic heart. Laced through with rock n' roll and literary iconography, the poet has pieced together his bleeding heart, and presented it in its persisting softness.

The genuine pumping of Wright's poetry, however, must not be mistaken for any putting on of airs. These are real, living memories here, not some passing occurrence, but persistent, embodied life. This is one of Rilke's prerequisites for even attempting to be a poet: "One must have memories of many nights of love . . . but one must also have been with the dying, have sat in a room with the dead and noises coming in at random." "And yet," Rilke says, "it is not yet enough to have memories. One has to be able to forget them. . . for it is not the memories in themselves that are worth the consequence. Only when they become the very blood within us, our every look and gesture, nameless and no longer distinguishable from our inmost self, only then, in the rarest of hours, can the first word of a poem arise in their midst and go out from among them."

Dan's *From Obscurity to Oblivion* is not a chivalrous narrative, but a retelling of the piss and grit that builds a man. He does not write the symbolic platitude of the reason or rime but the divisive desires of the soul. He doesn't remember his own life to enshrine it, but to lay bare earnesty for once in this new millennium. Who has not yearned to sit over coffee with their heroes? Who has not scribbled love notes fraught with self-doubt only to drop them off the DuSable Bridge?

As one who has sat for coffee with the author, himself having boarded many buses before with nothing but books in his hands, I implore you to follow advice from Hunter S. Thompson concerning this book in your hands: "Buy the ticket, take the ride."

Sincerely,

Katryn Dierksen
Founder of Bad Jacket Press
Author of *No More,*
Renaissance Man

PART 1:
WORKING BOHEMIAN'S BLUES
2008-2014

Working Bohemian's Blues

I have spit in the face of American Dreams
that did nothing
except take joy
in telling me
I was nothing more
than just another failure

I have grown up
seeing baby boomer addicts
neglect the children
they brought into this world
for the vain hope
that a second summer of love
would make them
eight miles high
once again

I've watched from the sidelines
as Gen Xers quote Townshend and Cobain like mantras
refusing to let us get started
while we scrape at the bottom
with holes in our clothes
holes in our shoes
and holes in our hearts

And what of us?

The next generation

a blank generation

that one without a style or grace

who do not have an identity to throw in your face

who work weekdays and weekends for an entire month

for a paycheck that's not even $100

and left to wonder how

to keep a car

keep a phone

keep warm

keep well fed

keep a roof over your head

keep peace of mind

keep from being left behind

as you try

to keep up with the frantic pace of life

out of fear

of being just another one

lost in the shuffle

as you're told you need all these and more

to even have a chance

at seeing tomorrow

Looking all around and wondering

where the reward is

They say real life starts

after you graduate high school

but in a world where

30, 40, 50, and 60

are all The New 20
it makes one feel doomed
to be a child forever
as they tell us to stop behaving
like the very children
they treat us as

Looking into a mirror
and hearing so many voices
real and imaginary
telling you
you need to have your life sorted out
Trying to climb the ladder of success
only to find
that at some point
somebody cut out the middle
Being told that you have to take
a leap of faith
to reach the other end
Watching as others try to make the jump
only to fall into the abyss
you spent a lifetime crawling out of

So confused as to what is life
and is it even worth living
Having all of this to deal with
plus looking for a job that'll support a wife and child
before making up my mind
on if I even want that in the first place

Wishing I had a clue
or two
as I drown amongst the absurdity of it all
as they call us all whiners, losers, failures, lazy
and every other damn insult they can think of
out of frustration
of no longer understanding
the same gripes
their generation once had

Working jobs and serving slobs
telling yourself
It's money in my pocket
so that's good enough for now
over and over
like some desperate consolation
Taking shit with a smile
being let go after awhile
because you don't fit in
you don't wear their grin
as you deal with a tornado in your head
that never stops
visiting that vicious cycle again
and again
and again
and again

Turning to friends who're always there
turning to the friends who you know will care

because they love
they live to love
and if it weren't for them
you could damn well be
somewhere below or above

Dealing with your 19th nervous breakdown of the day
and trying to hide it as best as you can
Doing your best
to make your way
Ignoring those who ignore your pleas
writing you off in their mind
by saying,
"That's life kid, get used to it"

Offering advice that attacks the symptoms
but never the sickness
while you scratch, claw, bawl
and fight on
to get through the passing days
seeing so-called adults
just as screwed up as yourself
maybe more
passing judgment and panicking in private
as life passes them by
Getting more and more childish
by the day
by the hour
by the moment

and you're left wondering
where was the happiness in a childhood
where you always felt
15 going on 35

And all you ever hear
is them telling you
you need
to grow up
and all you can say is
"How?"

Broken Bottles

There's too many drunks in this town
I say this because
there's too many broken bottles
littering the sidewalks,
triggering memories of a past
I'd much sooner forget.
Open doors now make my shoulders tense
and verbal attacks make me a mess.

I see at least one bus stop drunk
every couple of weeks
Pouring their bottles
of whiskey or vodka
or whatever the hell else they have
into empty water or juice bottles
they found in the trash
or on the sidewalk

Attempting to hit on
pretty young things
and making everyone else
around them nervous
because no one wants to deal
with the blind wrath of a drunk
trying to drink away all the problems
they feel the world
has given them

Making fools of themselves
by preaching advice no one wants
Who leave the evidence
of how desperate their souls really are
broken
littered across the sidewalk
for others to see and shake their heads at
and pretend they didn't notice.

Blaming the strangers who cross their path
Blaming everything that can never go back
Blaming this town in its glory and disgust
Making you feel at home
while ticking away like a mentally ill parent
who keeps you on edge
until you can't take it anymore

Is it my fate to be like these poor bastards?
Who have a bottle in one hand
and the hatred of the world in their eyes.
I already have one so is the other a matter of time?
One thing's for certain:
There's too many broken bottles
in this town

LWOP

Got off work early
and the time off
is worth more
than the paycheck
Getting away from the plastic town
with perfect people
with perfect teeth
perfect tans
and perfect houses
who always smile
like they got a damn coat hanger
in their mouth
I'm going to a place
where I can feel like myself
Amongst the decay of buildings boarded up,
with spray-painted warning
for crackheads to keep out.

Going down to see a friend in a coffee shop.
Spouting endless weird thoughts,
hoping for a laugh
or some other response.
Hoping I'm not too much of a nuisance.
Loving the immensity of the moment
and loving the feeling that maybe there's a place
in this damn town
where I belong.

Enjoying the time spent

with new friend

I've known for some time.

Finding a kindred spirit,

and hoping he believes

all the ways I see that we're alike.

Talking about nothingness

and how nothingness

is more important

to people like us

than everythingness.

Sticking around 'til closing time

to enjoy a walk

amongst a purple sunset

up and down Cherokee Street

and around Benton Park

until we decide it's time to call it a day

and I hitch a ride with him

back up to the county

Going back up north

from the lower city,

passing by the neon lights of downtown,

both professing a true love and devotion to the city,

and to living life to its fullest while we still have it

Stuck with a hot pizza on my lap,

hoping he's kind enough to offer me a slice

and he does

and he's so hungry himself
there's hardly enough left for Bill
by the time we get back.

Talking of loves that defined love for us,
sharing names,
times,
and admitting about the ones
who hurt us each so deeply
yet we'd still drop everything on our plates
if they ever asked us back
Talking so fast
our mouths moving faster
than the surrounding traffic
because there's too much to say
that it's impossible to stop

Sharing the visions we have,
the visions of the world we want to visit
Visions of England
Chicago
New York
Mexico
California
and a million other places
thought of by our restless souls
as we go on and on about music
funny observations
personal views on personal friends

and so much more
we barely pay attention
when it's time to get off
Highway 70

Soon making our way towards exit signs
and personal landmarks all too familiar.
Everything on Lindbergh
from the McDonald's near the Driver's Bureau
and all that follows
and we both know this stretch so well
we could close our eyes
and imagine each building as we pass it by
and know what's on
the other side

But seeing all this makes me sad
because I know it means
the turn to my street
is coming up
and so
as I make my way out of the car
I still say
it was worth more
than any paycheck

A Glimpse

Sometimes in life
you catch a glimpse
of what you think
would be perfect
The perfect life
the perfect partner
the perfect job
the perfect friend
A chance to see what would've happened
if the cards had been dealt
differently

They hardly ever all come at once
but they always leave you
reflecting on them
for the rest of your life
Picking and choosing the moments
that meant the most to you

Advice for a Confused Friend Who Already has the Answers

Never let them
lead you astray
Never go with the flow
when only suits everyone else
but you
Never settle
when you know your worth
Never pine for a past
that doesn't want you
Never keep the Devil in your loins
always keep him in your smile

You are a joy to behold
The world's coolest secret
And secrets are for keeping
Especially the good ones
Always smile like you know something
they don't
When they ask you what it is
Simply place your index finger
to your lips
and give 'em a wink

Comic books and other nonsense
are the key to true knowledge

The only conspiracies in this world are a joke
Have a good laugh at their expense
Within the world we make dark
There is always a sliver of light
With each smile and each laughter
The light grows brighter
And the day, just a little better

Random Thoughts from the Late Night

The aroma of pot is in the air
The fun tyme people are all dolled up
and out in full force
I could be one of them if I really wanted
If I didn't care
but I do care
I care too much
and that leads to overthinking
a skill I've mastered all too well
but need to stop.

I see the bums on 14th Street
all gather at the steamgrate
One of them tries to stop me
to get some change
but I keep on walking
She asks me where I'm going.
I say nothing
but in my mind, I reply
"mad"
as deadpan as I can.

The neon signs point to new gin joints
that pretend to be old.
The found souls
pretending to be lost.

I love and hate everything
about these cobblestone streets
with everything in me.
I hate that every time I open my mouth
my intellect shows up,
revealing me to be smarter
than even I know.
That's always when I'm told
I need to go back to an institution
I want nothing to do with.
Because it's a great lie.
Four to eight years of time and money
just to work the same job as someone with a GED.
Quite a good joke
when you think about it.

Intelligence is a desert island.
A door you can never reopen
once you go past.
Once third eyes are clean
facades can never be unseen

Union Square

Leaving New York today
and part of me doesn't want to go
Five days in a city that never sleeps
is just never enough
A farewell meal with friends in Williamsburg
and then I'm off
No tearful farewells at the airport
Just a payment to a cab driver
and then I'm out of this town

Leaving all those fantastic people
who made the trip worthwhile
and thinking about the heart I broke
who went back to England
Another regret to chalk up
to the fates not being in my corner
Wishing it could've been different
but knowing that a wish
won't change a damn thing

With an hour to kill
I watch the chess games in Union Square
and brace myself
for one final subway ride
to take the L back to Bedford Avenue
to the one place I found

a decent cup of coffee
at a decent fucking price

Wanting to feel paranoid in Manhattan
wanting to feel like the buildings
are out to kill me
telling me that next time
I won't be so lucky
Unimpressed and unmoved by me
Just another fucking tourist
in their eyes

But the thing is New York
I am unimpressed and unmoved
by you
You are not
your grand myth anymore
I'd have loved to have died
on your streets
but that doesn't seem
to be a badge of honor
anymore

Looking at the McDonald's and Barnes & Noble
and all the other billboard buildings
that surround me
and it all becomes too clear
I can't wait to get the fuck out of here

Leaving New York
and I can't fucking wait
Go fuck yourself New York
Maybe we'll meet again
under better circumstances

The Truest Friend

The best advice
is often what you already know
but you need somebody to tell you
And it is often
the truest friend
who
in the simplest language
will tell you
what you need
to know

To the Gut

(A Poem for Ellen Hilton Cook)

To the gut
To the point
To the limit of how far
you know
you can push yourself
Face your demons
look them right in the eye
and take them on
like a motherfucker

To the gut
To the point
To have the courage to go
to the darkest corners of a mind
that you're too scared
to spend too much time in

To the gut
To know you're not going to waste
your time or theirs
with unnecessary
bullshit

To the point
To get where it is

you know you want to go
and to be able to have fun
with the language
while getting there

To the gut
To the point
To feel a need to get something out
because you'll go mad otherwise
because it's something so scary
so pure
so true
it could only come
from the heart

PART 2:
MURDER CITY SPECIAL
2014–2017

A Preface

I write
because I suffer from the confusion
of not knowing what other people think
I write because I know
that if I keep writing
line for line
that eventually
I'll hit a bullseye on the dartboard
One line
that will ring true one hundred years from now
That is true immortality

I write because I feel too bohemian for my own good
a mess losing money faster than I make it
I write because my brain loves to go off on tangents
Wondering if every microwave meal
will bring me one step closer to cancer

I write
because nothing in this world
is a wasted moment
I write to satisfy a voice in my head
that never shuts up
I write because it's the only thing that will make me feel
like I accomplished something
no matter how many hours I worked at a job that day

I write for the clichés and truths
I write for hopeless romantic hearts
and on occasion
myself
and most of the time
I write at the bar
because that's where
I can see the world best

Murder City Special

Truth slingshots me
back to the beginning
and I'm left
with nothing
but thoughts
of everyday suicides
and one too many imaginary exits
I could have taken
instead
of the one too many realities
I face each day

Tired of Hip Street politics
death looms in every headline
murder
shootings
nuclear fallout
another Murder City Special
served up straight

Pushing yourself
in experiments to see
where your limits are
loose lips sink ships
ruin immature lives
Feeling nothing but tired

and bare
as the party was over long ago
the Edge of Cliffs
talk shit behind your back
and in front of your face

Fever dreams run rampant
People tell you truths
you swear are false
and now
you question each step
each ring
each breath
each memory
It'd be so easy
to resign yourself
to what you know
sit at the bar
order a Murder City Special
beer
shot
smoke
and watch the world go by

Sometimes
when you're ready to reform
to leave bad habits behind
the world will do everything in its power
to keep you from doing so

because if you're a fuck up
it can point at you
And still feel allowed
to be a fuck up too

When your best ain't enough
but your resilience won't let you quit
you're stuck
you're stuck between the devil and the deep blue sea
while the line between
boredom
and killing yourself
leads to purgatoried torsos
and livers feeling the stress of the job
and you swear that the names and faces you know
beside and behind you
are all having a much better time than you
as you stare at your drink
Murder City Special
straight up

The Sounds of a City

The sounds of a city
are of winners and beggars
Lovers kissing in the rain
feeling a new love for a first time
and the broken hearted
screaming out from windows
and rooftops
of street corner dwellers
hitting on the girl of the moment
of those who die in alleys
while someone on their smoke break
watches from across the way
Of the well-dressed crowd
eating outside
and of the legless veteran
who has lost it all

The rumbling of an elevated train
The few seconds of overheard conversation
spoken in a million different languages
The beat of worn tennis shoes
hitting pavement
because a journey's not done yet
The wail of a siren
racing after saints and sinners alike
The profanities of suburban yuppies

getting too drunk again in the latest neon hot spot
only to go home to preach
about how dangerous
downtown really is

The sounds of a city
are a million heartbeats
going all at once

Chasing the Ghosts of My Idols

Boarding a bus
at 5:49
in the morning
heading downtown
to make coffee
for the next eight hours
Barely awake

I still don't know
the difference
between a good relationship
and a bad one
Maybe there is none
Either way
I always feel like I'm in the way
Too many great artists
putting stuff out there
All I ever do is sit at home
hate the world
and love it just as much

No luck
No love
No time
The more I read
the more I know

life is just an endless cycle
of the same bullshit
I've yet to read a writer
who told me something about life
I didn't already know
Life becomes a habit
you want to kick
but it always keeps you
like a losing gambler

I see Ginsberg in my eyes
Bukowski in my beer
Kerouac in my heart
and Thompson in my head
There's Vonnegut in my smile
and Burroughs beneath the gravestone
I wish anyone of them
were still alive
to talk to
Sometimes you need more
than a friend's reassurance
that you're not wasting
your time

God's in the Jukebox

I overheard a man say
as I was walking out
of the grocery store
that God is alive
and hiding
in the jukeboxes
around the world

I laughed to myself
about the notion
but then I thought
there could be some validity
to that

The old saying goes
that ninety percent
of the people on this planet
wound up with the wrong person
and that's what keeps
the jukebox spinning

People keep looking
for truths
for answers
and there's no greater
truth

or answer

than the ones inside

a good song

Even the ones

that seem to be

about nothing

because sometimes

another person's nothing

is all we need

Hunting with Hemingway

My grandfather once told me
that he knew Ernest Hemingway
because my grandfather's uncle
would go hunting with him
and sometimes he would bring my grandfather along
"Most sullen man I ever met," my grandfather said.
"Someone should've done that man a favor
and shot him before he shot himself!"

"If anyone shot more than he did
he'd get depressed and drink.
If they all went out hunting without him
he'd get depressed and drink.
When his hunting buddies refused to call him Papa
he'd get depressed and drink.
And when he ran out of booze
he'd get depressed
steal a friend's bottle
and then he'd drink."

Some say the real reason he shot himself
was that one day
he was out of friends
out of booze
and too lazy
to go to the damn store
I can sympathize

Red

I wasn't looking for it
I wasn't on the make
but like everything else in life
you don't look for
it just happened
like a perfect storm
She said one thing
I said another
Then she read to me
her favorite Bukowski poem
and then I knew
all bets were off

So here I sit
by myself
her smile on my mind
Trying to play it cool
laughing
because I don't fool myself
I can't stop smiling
Fighting the urge
of wanting to be someone else
because deep down
I know I'm not the kind of guy
she tends to go for

I still look forward
to the next time
our paths cross
hoping I can do anything
that makes her want
to be closer to me

In the meantime
I pick up the book
her favorite Bukowski poem
is in
one I overlooked
too many times
but now
I can't get enough of
I hear her voice
when I read it
and still
I can't stop smiling
although I know
this probably won't end well

Scenes from a Sunday Morning

Got a headache
while heading to work
Can't tell if it's a migraine
or a hangover
If this is getting older
to hell with it
At the very least
give me back the liver
I had at 25

Looking out the window
staring at the boarded-up buildings
on Broadway
Seeing ghosts of prosperity
killed by reality
Baseball-capped drunks
getting the first tall boy
of the day
and starting things
off right

I ask myself where I fit
in my own story
sometimes I feel the lead
sometimes an extra

Don't know if I've got
a chance in hell
what's worse
I don't know if I want one

Getting off the bus
on Washington Avenue
and I feel
like I'm in a different world
I look up at the lofts
on second, third, and seventeenth story floors
too rich for my blood
and feel a sense
that I'm supposed to want to aspire
to live
in such posh lodgings
I'd only want
a place like that
if I knew I could fuck it up
for myself

A Larry Rice refugee
asks me for a dollar
I give it to him
remembering what it was like
to sit on a park bench
with no home to go to
and a cop car slowing down
to wonder what I'm doing

The biggest injustice
you can put on a person
is not allowing them a chance
to rest their feet
So many old classmates
can still go home
when life leaves them with nothing
I don't have that option

I walk into the coffee shop
I used to work at
and everyone says
that since I'm clean shaven
I must have gotten laid
I didn't
but I'll let them think I did

I down the ibuprofen and espresso
I came in for
and go to work to open the shop
Another day, another dollar
another look over my shoulder
to see the wolf
patiently waiting by the door

Rose Tinted Glasses

She wants the past
in a nice, neat package
To take the good
but the leave the bad
to a blind eye

I look at the news
I see race riots
a people protesting for equality
news of a war that never seems to end
debates about a woman's right to her own body
and an ever-present pissing contest
between the West and Russia
and the left and the right

"Weren't the sixties so great!"
she says, wistfully
"I'd give anything
to have lived then!"

Heart

Nobody wants a heart
that feels so deeply
because when it breaks
it still hurts
as fresh
and as deep
as the first cut
you ever had

You can try to drown it
You can try to run from it
You can try to forget it
But there it'll always sit
waiting for you to face it
and shed the first
of many truthful tears

Tears shed
for old school overtures
now made silly after thoughts
for old souls drinking themselves insensitive
and waking with hate and rage in the morning
Lost in confusion
and contradiction

But the older you get

even through the worst pains

that make it hard

to listen to music

or to even exhale

you're glad

your heart can still feel

as deeply

and truly

as it does

Thanksgiving is the Loneliest Holiday

Thanksgiving is the loneliest holiday
when the only thing to keep you company
is the mouse
you hear
scratching through the wall
and your dinner
is a bottle
of wild turkey

You hear through the grapevine
of all the Friendsgivings
that people you know
are having
but you weren't invited to
as you try to call family
in and out of town
who all have plans
You want to speak up
ask why you weren't invited
but the ones in town
don't answer

The only people
who contact you
are the bored wife
who tries to fuck you

behind her husband's back
to say she wishes
she was with you
so you could be inside her
and her husband
who found your number
to tell you
to do the world a favor
and kill yourself
At least they cared
enough to call

With each swig
you can hear the mouse
try harder and harder
to make it's way through the wall
you wish it could be different
like when you were younger
spending Thanksgiving with family
but there's no room
for family
for the working class
at least not this weekend

The Lowest Level of Fame

They always come up to me
when I'm trying to relax
and talk with my friends
They tell me that they saw me read
and oh, how amazing I was
and that maybe
if I wasn't too busy
I could read their stuff
sometime
telling me the same opening lines
five times in a row
Caught in the allure
of the lowest level of fame
known to man

I wonder what they'd do
if they found out
how much of a nothing
I really am
That I have no job
and nothing to my name
except a good reputation
that fades
with each day
of unemployment

But despite my discomforts
they go on
unaware or uncaring
about how good I am
and how it'd mean the world
to them
for me
to read the words
of a total stranger

St. Louis Fireworks

I hear the helicopters
over my head
and hear the St. Louis fireworks
It's always 4th of July
down here
They're always off
somewhere in the distance
followed by the sirens
The distance you hear them from
and how many you hear
is the barometer
on if you should go back inside
or if you want to take a chance
and walk the streets alone

I guess I've just gotten used to it
and have tuned it out
and just go on my way
But there's always that fear
of being in the wrong place
at the wrong time
and getting caught in a crossfire
Some street level entropy
seeing something
that you'll never un-see

I try to do my best though

making the most of each new day

and every time I'm so close

to forgetting about that particular worry

I hear them again

off in the distance

pop

pop

pop

and hope

that I'll be able to make it home that night

A Feast of Friends

With faces you've seen
once and a thousand times
from days and nights spent
at the corner
of Virginia and Cherokee
Drunken nights
of euphoria
and our own
moveable feast

Pinball in the corner
that makes the most annoying sound
when you get an extra ball
and a jukebox blaring
that inspires the most enthusiastic
off-key singing
you've ever heard
Walking through a door
to one of the great nights
of your life
Finding at least one person
you recognize
they offer to buy you a shot
and then you're off
to the races
while friends drink

their mason jar drinks
and sing to each other
the songs they bought
to coast through the night
With moments better
than any fiction
Fueled by coffee in the morning
beer in the afternoon
and whiskey at night
Moments that mean smiles
to those who were there
Conversations lost
to time and hangovers
Seeing the old souls and traveling sound machines
Barflys and functioning alcoholics
Walking pop culture encyclopedias
Scenes
intermingling with each other
and
...oh yeah...
some guy named Al

Spider web tree branches
becoming dreamcatchers
under the streetlight
Trouble houses
down the cobblestone street
Cherokee bums
asking for a dollar

from anyone hanging outside
or walking to their car
and no end to anything
ever
except
last call

Midnight Hour

The midnight hour
bring the heartaches
that are the sweetest little heartaches
you've ever felt
when the one you care for
talks of others
describing you as their perfect match
but never bothers to put
two and two together

But it doesn't matter
you leave it aside
to share a special moment
with that special someone
letting them go on
as long as they need to
no matter how much
it might tear you apart inside

When it's done
you go outside
light a cigarette
enjoying and regretting

the sweet little heartaches of life

and wishing

that life

would tweak itself

just a little bit

Dreams

They say that in dreams
are where responsibilities begin
I guess then
that even in dreams
you're never really free

I stare at a sun
that seems angry with me
The beers in this town say
I got a problem
But the cigarettes say
I'm doing just fine
All the blank pages
have the nerve
to call me a hack
That I should just give up the dream
my dream
the only thing
my heart knows how to do right

As California slides into the ocean
and Missouri drowns in the mud
I lay myself down
and wait for the predicted flood
dreaming
of how I got so close

but dreams
are always
out of touch
I guess that's why
they're always
the only thing
we're left with

The Beast

Romantic two-faced human growth
throwing up flowers
from Van Gogh face
taking in unknown pleasures
for sake of wildest fantasies
Jekyll and Hyde
with the possibility of Bob, Ted, Carol, and Alice
Lucifer lungs
under Parisian blue angel sky
keeping Shakespeare company

Hookah beast
from children's story
darkest undertones
with kindest heart
wanting elusive love
it cannot get
from itself
romantic's heart
will of the forgotten
determined to eschew
damnation

Sad Eyes

Sad eyes
of a beautiful woman
made just another
face in the crowd
by too many other
beautiful women

Blue cotton sundress
Brown hair
that shines in the sun
she never looks a person in the eyes
when passing
as they nod
to offer the politest
hello
they can offer a stranger

Sad eyes
hidden behind Annie Hall smile
Sad eyes
longing for companionship
Sad eyes
not knowing
what they're sad about
Sad eyes
on a beautiful face
that are never ever
seen

Muse

She doesn't belong on a mountain top
nor a pedestal
She is not the answer
to all your troubles
or even the cause of them
Do not make her the muse
she is not
Do not make her more
than her imperfections
but still love her
for the light she brings

Vicious stabs from thorns
will make her stab with a glance
all with the poise and grace
of a lady
with a drink in hand
and pain in grip
as true love leaves no traces

She avoids Errol Flynn monsters
who try to fit agendas
with courtships
that lead straight
to Emily Post depressions

Sweet words
leave a bitter taste
until proven true
Do not call her a goddess
Do not call her a queen
Do not promise moments
that are beyond your reach

Do not give her a role
Do not tell her the lines
she must read
Love her as a friend
Love her as a woman
Love her as a human being
Do not make her the muse
she is not
Let only her love
inspire you
if and when
the time comes

Untitled Poem from the End of a Long Day

Graffiti walls burn down niceties
as neon lights hide pretensions
Wage slaves search for identity
as they feel like working class heroes
amongst so-called geniuses
and feel like geniuses amongst
so-called working-class heroes

The dollar that hypnotizes you
Loses power
when it cannot buy anything
Mind traps run fierce
as amateur psychics grow angry
swearing they just told you everything
without opening their mouths
People unqualified to speak for the world
yell at nothing
because they refuse to comprehend
that some people don't have lofty goals

Some people
just want to be left alone

If Movies Are to Be Believed

If movies are to be believed
good guys always win
and bad guys always lose

If movies are to be believed
telling a woman that you're immortal
and were born in the highlands of Scotland
400 years ago
will always get you in to their pants

If movies are to be believed
preaching to the converted
will always get the job done
The slimy little asshole
who you want to get theirs
will always get theirs
and you can rely on your friends
to never let you down

If movies are to be believed
you can afford to be idyllic
because justice will always be served

If movies are to be believed
you can trust your parents
unless they're stepparents

who have bad skin
and look evil

You can trust the cops
especially the ones
that follow their own rules
because authority figures
will never lie to you
right?

If movies are to be believed
it all works out
another happen ending
nothing to worry about
fade to black

Bag of Clothes

She texted me out of nowhere
in the middle of the night
like a dream
and in many ways
it still feels like it was
A year of knowing each other
a year of build up
to finally say and do
all we wanted

It didn't last long
but from St. Patty's Day to Easter
I was allowed to be the romantic I wanted to be
instead of the loner I usually am
The first night we fucked
she quoted Jane Austen
to tell me she loved me
Aware that I was looking for a lifetime lover
but she was just looking for a room

She invited me to spend
every moment I was free
to be with her
only to tell me
I was coming on too strong
Maybe I was

In the end,
who did what doesn't matter to anyone
what's done is done
Though if it came down to it
we'd both be first in line
to tell you all the ways
we're both fucked up

Memories get more faded each day
and the only proof
she was ever here
was the bag of clothes
she left behind

Write a Poem About It

Sometimes
life's too rough
to put pen to paper

Sometimes
you don't want
to share your pain
with the world that day

Sometimes
you just want to vent
your daily vent

Sometimes
you just want to know
a friend's shoulder
is there

Clichés and Stereotypes

Let the poet's heart
not be clubbed into submission
Never let it believe that writing
at best
is a lonely life
Let it be free
to paint on the canvas
of the mind's eye

Let not a poet
drink themselves to death
with the furniture polish
they bought that morning
Let them show you beauty
as only they can
Let them show you haunted truths
romantic nature
The passion and intellect
that only they have

No Reason

You never know when that feeling will hit
but you know it when it comes
When a wave washes over you
and you know,
the person you're with
won't be around much longer
You try to fight against it
because this person
hasn't done anything wrong
For no reason at all
you just don't love them anymore

You try to rationalize with your feelings,
trying to not draw attention to the matter
because the more a significant other
asks what's wrong
the more they accidentally annoy you
and fuel the argument of your emotions

You remind yourself of every good memory
but even that feels forced
So you stop trying to convince yourself
And keep secretly hoping that everything
might work out different for a change

You try to hold your lover close
though your smothering of them
causes them to push you away
and soon your smothering of them
makes you feel smothered
and you push them away

They don't know how to react
and you don't know what to say
without sounding insane
so instead you say nothing
as a relationship remains
damaged enough to decay

And there's nothing to blame
because you didn't want this
you didn't plan this
but a feeling just sprung up
for no reason

Real Poets Don't Wear Rolling Stones T-Shirts

Click the pen
Begin again
JJF smile
Just another freak
in the freak kingdom
Black t-shirt
Ripped jeans
clean by default
Zippo flicks open
Flame rises
Smoke inhaled

Don't give two shits about theory
Never paid attention to what I was taught
Ritalin helped with that
Down here
with hippies, drunks, rainbows
children of the sun, moon and earth
All of us light years from home
and we like it that way

We all flew into the sun
some were burned
some were phoenixes
we've spun the spider's web

we got stuck on where to go next
we drank too much Stag and PBR
Creative cold feet
is just code for "not good enough"
with "didn't wanna sell out"
being the bullshit you sell yourself

Too much time
thinking about past mistakes
to prevent future ones
Insides become a mess
when someone makes you feel something
that's not love
but is just as pure

Xanax and cigarettes before the gold rush
discover secret histories
of smalltown kings
as the man onstage
takes off his pants
to shock you
because revelation
is all he has left

Piss poor piano plays
nickels at a time
Mozart never had to do this shit
Those unable to do it themselves
tell you how you should do it better

Those who try so hard to fit in
never know when to shut up
Shoot me up
get me off
Do we want love anymore
or just incestuous friendships
that comfort us just enough
So far from truth
So close to hope
Superheroes are real
when you believe in them

There is no end
There is only when you leave
Click the pen
Begin again

Bullies

Timely thoughts
on timeless problem
Bad guys win the day
Parents can't look children in the eye
Science and fact
now shots in the dark

David Byrne raps
now prove prophecy
as puppets dance for freedom
Children keep responsibilities
only to be ignored
Lunch money stolen
as necessary hostage
They'd shoot you in the street
bragging that they got away with it
and then claim they never did it
because they don't remember

Pornography preached against
by those who read the National Review
but only for the articles
Transcontinental snobs become uneasy
when called out for what they are

Immigration gets blamed on abortion
as they wish for a government
small enough to drown in the tub
while judges are impaled
Six steps forward
means ten steps back
Brass rings are never meant to be touched

Obscenity normalized
too many problems swept under the rug
as they wonder why the house is so dusty
So many scramble for every dollar
unaware they may not have a world to spend it in

Talking heads scream for most attention
Here we go again
The point is never understood the first time
because there never is one

Floating

Unable to touch the ground
memories won't give the facts
Grip lost
Too late to investigate
Childlike mistakes
question worth

Passion refuses to understand love
Numbed lips search for words
Best intentions
lead straight to the briar patch
Sleepwalk pays rent
Wishes reach for certainty
Confusion in eyes says all

Don't start what you can't finish
Moments make the difference
Impatience moves time
the same speed
as everything else

Love Shines Through

There will still be days
where love shines through
when the chaos will subside
There will still be days
when power chords ring out without reverb
and the day will be yours to enjoy

Warmth can still greet you
even after the groundhog sees its shadow
Be the one to lift a smile
at a fellow traveler
even when there's not a smile in you
There will still be days
when love shines through

Portrait

(Dedicated to the memory of Shelley A. Wright, 1958 - 2007)

I recall opening a drawer
and seeing old notebooks
with your handwriting
unmistakable
written in poetry
seeing glimpses of your young heart
and always wondering
if you wanted the world
with the same yearning I have for it
and wonder what might have been for you
if I hadn't come along

I step into the old house
always too small for a family of four
with two dogs no less
and even smaller now
for a single man
Looking around the empty living room
and remembering where everything used to be
the couches and televisions
we went through
over the years
seeing where the old recliner used to be
the old recliner that you sat in
during your final months
in a constant pain

that tore us up inside as well
because we could not stop your pain
Thinking of a stepfather
revising history after your death
making me the disappointment
by telling tales
of the happy homemaker
you never were
and only seeing you
as an angel
once you'd gone to Heaven
Losing myself in too many tears
as ghosts of one too many head games
come at me
as memories played on a constant loop
that get at me
in a way
no one in my present
knows how to get at me

Closing my eyes to get away from the mind terrors
I open my eyes and find myself in Chicago
on Winchester
walking in the same footsteps
as you did so many years ago
when your water broke
starting on Montrose and walking two blocks
to Wilson
to the hospital where I was born

and where so many memories still sit
one block over
in that six-family house
unaware that you're never coming back

Memories of sisters
calling you Nother Mother
when a parent was not there
Memories of a drunken father
drinking away golden opportunities
for the sake of another drink
Memories of a mother
stretched to her limits
taking care of five children
however many pets
and a part time husband

Going back over to Montrose
and seeing the bank you worked at
when you met my father
and thinking of the double-edged sword that was
Grateful for my birth
but knowing the hurt
that son of a bitch
would cause you

Leaving you in debt
Leaving you confused
Leaving you in the hospital

and letting you come home to an apartment
as empty as the love he had for you
without the courtesy of a note
after a ten-month relationship
nine of which I was in the womb
only call from Texas
two weeks later
to let you know things just weren't working out

Spending time with him
at his insistence
during the youngest years of my life
whenever we'd go back up to Chicago
and him taking me on the errands he had to run
never taking the time
to talk with the child
he had decided to abandon
Memories of dive bars where he needed to get money
of blues clubs he wanted to play
and old men jamming amongst a sea of empty chairs
letting me strum the guitars
they were playing
with my index finger
and being drawn
to that angelic noise
that would wind up calling to me
for a lifetime

Remembering the last time I ever saw him
You taking me to Lambert airport

because he had a layover
and he demanded to see "his boy"
and me not wanting to see him
because it finally began to dawn on my young mind
just what he had done to you
That his family didn't even think I was his
and the times I cried myself to sleep
wondering why he never thought
I was ever worth
a dime of acknowledgment
Thinking of the times as a grown man
I had looked him up
and thought I'd found him
only to be told by a machine
he didn't want to listen to my area code
only to dip deeper
to find he died in September
when I was thirteen
I guess in the end
Papa really was a rolling stone

Knowing of the times I heard you cry
behind closed doors
for unknown reasons
from adolescence to adulthood
wishing there was anything that I could do for you
wondering if it was my fault
Thinking of all the times
you heard good music

coming from my room
and would walk over to open the door
just a little wider
than the crack I'd left it at
to ask me questions about what I was listening to
and you smiling and laughing
at my enthusiasm in talking about music
It's not often a child gets their parent in to Ozzy

Knowing the frustration I was
giving you report cards
marked with C's, D's and F's
not because I was stupid
I just never saw the point in doing the work
Because I knew what I wanted to do
The hardest thing
about being an old soul
is waiting 18 years
for people to acknowledge you as a legal adult
and waiting ten more years
for anyone
to respect what the hell
you have to say

Feeling your strength
which kept everyone you knew
feel safe
Your strength
which was the pillar that held so much together

Your strength

in the face of everything

The story you told me

of the girl in high school who was mad

that the guy she liked

liked you

and so she pulled you

by the hair

in a Chicago alley

where she and her two friends

beat you up

but still you wouldn't go down without swinging

Showing me the scars on your knuckles

from that time

and from when you and your sisters

my aunts

dealt with anyone

who called Uncle Kevin

a dreaded word

that began with R

because of his handicap

because of his wheelchair

because his mind wasn't what the rest of the world

wanted it to be

The time you barged into my middle school

demanding to speak to the teacher

who said I had horrible taste in literature

because everything I read

was made into a movie

Your strength

that helped you get through

the alcoholic men in your life

a father

lovers

a husband

Your strength

that helped you through so much

Your strength

that disappeared

when you resigned yourself

to your illness

Remembering you teaching me

when I was old enough

how to keep you from biting your tongue

if ever the epilepsy you fought your whole life

were to suddenly strike you

Remembering you collapsing in the hallway

Silent

unmoving

Thinking quick to call 911

Scared at the age of eight

that I almost lost you

Remembering at eleven

taking my brother

who was three at the time

in the other room

as stress and sunstroke

caused you to have a fit
trying to take his mind
and mine
off from what I knew was happening
in the living room
while our grandmother dealt with you
and brought you down from where you were
too many times before

Your memory comes to me
at the oddest of times
Your memory comes to me
as much now as then
Ten years after your bones were laid to rest
Your memory tells me
I need to be better than I am
Your memory leaves me alone
To be my own man
Your memory
Your memory
Your memory

These memories
which are all in every memory of you
as I say a prayer
and hope it's heard somewhere
All of this
in the memory of you
my mother
whose name is Shelley

Forgotten Songs

I wish I could've written
all the beautiful songs
that get forgotten
I could've made a career
out of such gems
I would've taken care of them
I would've made sure
they were heard
even after the month-long band
they were written for
broke up

I play along to them
in private
I imagine an alternative life
playing along to songs
that only twenty people know
Songs who were dismissed
by their creators
as not good enough
and I think
maybe it wasn't the songs

The Death of the Ladies Man

No woman is good enough
Though he falls in love
twenty times a day
He feels confident in taking whatever comes along
until the love of his life shows up
But one day
he'll wake up
incapable of showing love
with a heart that's no longer a heart
but just a ball of duct tape
with the remains inside
grounded down
to a fine powder

He'll carry himself with a Cary Grant posture
he'll flash a Sean Connery smile
he'll drink with a Humphrey Bogart attitude
he'll look straight to a heart with Clark Gable eyes
but none of that will matter to him
He'll only pay attention to the cries
no one will hear
as the only people
able to make him feel anything
are the ones
he's already loved

He'll always enjoy the moment
of a new woman
enjoying the verbal dance
but as beauty kisses bruises
he knows what will come
in the morning
That he won't be
as emotionally available as he thought

She'll do her best
to not appear hurt by the fact
that he's no different
and then two people
who deserve love
will be hurt
once again

They'll both go off in search of a lie
they can turn into a truth
They'll both sit alone
they'll both look away
they'll both have different answers
for what went wrong with themselves
and others
She'll get phone calls
she doesn't want to answer
He'll answer a phone call
that'll do

The callers will pine for them

waiting for the day the world can love again

and everyone will drink

and everyone will wonder

why people don't accept the love

that they deserve

and every ladies man knows

they're just another fuck boi gigolo

and life goes on

without them

The Age of the Argument

There is too much to do
and we want to do it all
See everything in the world
in a nanosecond
just to forget what we've seen
Phone numbers are now
only to be stored and forgotten

Wary social commentary
an old folks game
Century old cries for change
a backdrop for the girls and boys
Intelligence puts on false heirs
that the rest of the world
doesn't care about
as now our greatest fear
is only to be proven wrong

It's the age of the argument
and no one's taken debate class

First Date

"Oh, so you're a writer," she said
"So, what are you gonna write about our date?"
"I don't know if I'm going to," I said
"Aren't I worth writing about?" she asked,
pouting,
taking a step near the edge
of baby talk.
"I'll be the judge of that," I quipped.
"You should write about me!" she said.
"Maybe," I said coyly.

She spent the rest of the night
trying to be funny
telling me a lot about herself
and being playfully over dramatic

We went back to my place
messed around a little
and when I asked her
a few days later
if she wanted to go
on a second date
She said "no"

I guess in the end,
she got what she wanted
I wound up writing about her
after all

What a Feeling Means

They sparked each other's soul
and it felt so great
So great
that they had to hide it
because great passion
and great love
are viewed in their world
as poison

A day earlier
they barely knew each other
but now they felt something
they hadn't felt
for so long
it scared them

He looked over at her
and knew
that if they'd met a little earlier
in life
everything would be fine
She looked at him
wondering how he could've gotten
under her skin
so well

And both wondered
if they were crazy
for feeling what they felt

She went to the bathroom
to wipe away tears
and compose herself
He snuck around
to clean up a few things in his room
Although she'd already seen
the mess his room was
he thought a little more effort
couldn't hurt

She thought herself silly
He thought himself stupid
They both looked at the clock
4:17
She asked if she could stay the night
hoping she didn't sound too awkward
He said it'd be fine
Holding back his enthusiasm
She snuggled up to him
He put his arm around her
They both wondered
how something so strange
could feel like home

Last Call

In seas of whiskey
Sitting with nighthawks and mad dogs
Days that move faster
than the speed of magic
Friends smoked
down to the filter and buds
with faint images
of silver naked ladies

A true America
a false hope
Land stretched to the line of boredom
Too many nights
out of sight
out of mind
Too many open roads
with too many exits to anywhere
and lot lizard love

No one wants a hard life
but there's no use bitching
about what you can't control
Shit
Two tears in a bucket
motherfuck it

Happy Ending

I wish I could give you a happy ending
I wish I could give you pretty little lies
I wish I could show the joy
felt through the shittiest of climates

I wish that I knew that you knew
No matter how low the soul
The spirit can still soar
I wish I could show you
every chance one has
to kiss the sky
before bumming on a skid row art street

I wish I could give you a happy ending
that wasn't fairy tales and bullshit
because I love you more than that
I wish I knew how to give you a chance
to experience the wonder of the cosmos
by seeing the wonder of the Earth

I wish I knew how to keep my big mouth
from getting me in to trouble
I wish I could talk to you
like I used to be able to do
I wish I had more to talk about
than just what was on my mind in that moment

I wish I could give you a happy ending
I wish I could show the silver lining
in every darkness
and I wish it could be true
so we could both believe it

Daniel W. Wright is an award-nominated poet and fiction writer. He most recently was a co-editor on *Strange Tales from Cherokee Street: An Anthology of St. Louis Poets* (Spartan Press, 2022) and wrote the foreword for *Sacred Decay: The Art of Lauren Marx* (Dark Horse, 2021). He is the author of eight collections of poetry, including *Love Letters from the Underground* (Spartan Press, 2021), *Rodeo of the Soul* (Spartan Press, 2019), and *Murder City Special* (Bad Jacket, 2017). His work has appeared in print journals such as *The Literary Parrot, BUK100, 365 Days,* and *Gasconade Review,* as well as online journals such as *Book of Matches.* He currently resides in St. Louis, MO, where you can usually find him in a bar or a bookstore.

This project was made possible, in part, by generous support from the Osage Arts Community.

Osage Arts Community provides temporary time, space and support for the creation of new artistic works in a retreat format, serving creative people of all kinds — visual artists, composers, poets, fiction and nonfiction writers. Located on a 152-acre farm in an isolated rural mountainside setting in Central Missouri and bordered by ¾ of a mile of the Gasconade River, OAC provides residencies to those working alone, as well as welcoming collaborative teams, offering living space and workspace in a country environment to emerging and mid-career artists. For more information, visit us at www.osageac.org

Osage Arts Community